WEDGES

Louise Spilsbury

PowerKiDS
press.

New York

Published in 2019 by The Rosen Publishing Group
29 East 21st Street, New York, NY 10010

Copyright © 2019 by The Rosen Publishing Group

Produced for Rosen by Calcium Creative Ltd
Editors for Calcium Creative Ltd: Sarah Eason and Harriet McGregor
Designer: Paul Myerscough
Picture researcher: Rachel Blount

Illustration by Geoff Ward

Picture credits: Cover: Shutterstock: Free Video Photo Agency; Inside: Shutterstock:
AndrUa: p. 18; Hans Christiansson: p. 7; CREATISTA: p. 5; Designua: p 6; Emma Dumitrescu:
p. 24; Krisztian Farkas: p. 20l; Freevideophotoagency: p. 13; lorenzo Gambaro: p. 10;
Thomas Holt: p. 19; Irakite: pp. 1, 4; Josfor: p. 22; A Katz: p. 17; Marinat197: p. 8;
PickOne: pp. 3, 9; Pro3DArtt: p. 23; Thomas Soellner: p. 11; Steny02: p. 29; David
Tadevosian: p. 16; Tkyszk: p. 12; Toiletroom: p. 15r; Alexandr Tolstoy: pp. 20-21;
VanderWolf Images: p. 28; Rubanov Vladimir: p. 25; Wikimedia Commons: MCSN Liam
Kennedy: pp. 26-27; U.S. Coast Guard: pp. 14-15; U.S. Navy photo by Photographer's
Mate Airman Carl E. Gibson: p. 27t.

Cataloging-in-Publication Data

Names: Spilsbury, Louise.
Title: Wedges / Louise Spilsbury.
Description: New York : PowerKids Press, 2019. | Series: Technology in action | Includes
glossary and index.
Identifiers: LCCN ISBN 9781538337660 (pbk.) | ISBN 9781538337653 (library bound) |
ISBN 9781538337677 (6 pack)
Subjects: LCSH: Wedges--Juvenile literature.
Classification: LCC TJ1201.W44 S67 2019 | DDC 621.8'11--dc23

Manufactured in the United States of America

CPSIA Compliance Information: Batch CSPK18: For further information, contact Rosen Publishing, New York, New York, at 1-800-237-9932.

Contents

Machines and Forces

Machines are all around us! We use machines every day in many different ways. When you open a door or slice a piece of toast, you are using a machine. Machines are tools that help us do **work**.

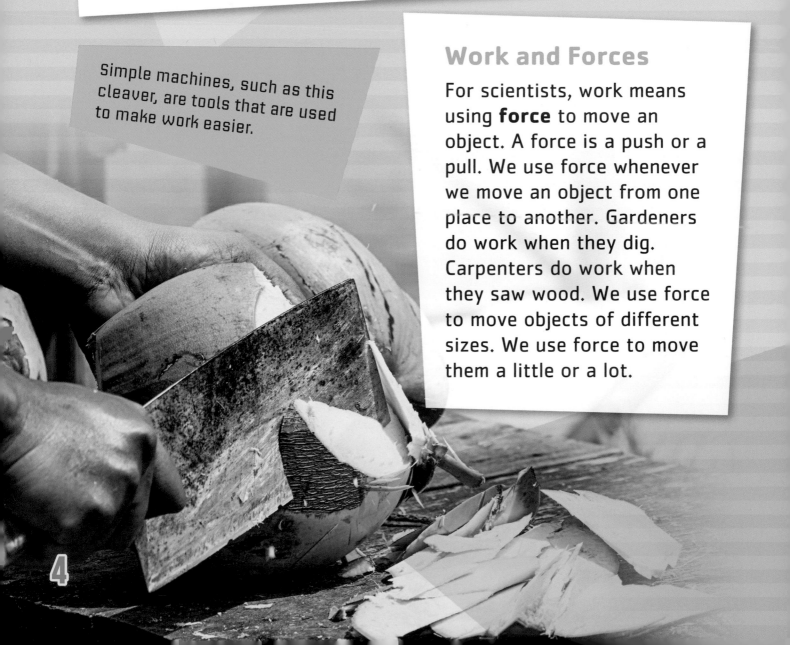

Simple machines, such as this cleaver, are tools that are used to make work easier.

Work and Forces

For scientists, work means using **force** to move an object. A force is a push or a pull. We use force whenever we move an object from one place to another. Gardeners do work when they dig. Carpenters do work when they saw wood. We use force to move objects of different sizes. We use force to move them a little or a lot.

Simple Machines

Machines make work easier or faster by increasing the strength or the **direction** of a force. Some machines are complicated and have many moving parts. Other machines have few or no moving parts. They are so simple that people do not think of them as machines. There are six types of simple machines: the inclined plane, the wedge, the screw, the lever, the wheel and axle, and the pulley. Let's take a look at some simple machines in action: wedges.

This machete is being used to chop down bushes. It is a type of wedge.

How Wedges Work

A wedge is a tool that pushes two edges apart. It is triangular in shape. It is thick at one end and narrows to a thin edge at the other end. An example of a wedge is an ax.

Single and Double Wedges

A wedge can be a single wedge or a double wedge. A single wedge has one sloping surface, such as a doorstop. A double wedge has two sloping surfaces or sides. The sides look like two **ramps**, or inclined planes, positioned back to back. An ax head is a double wedge.

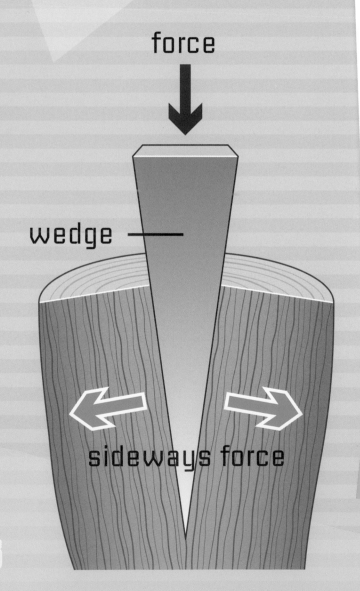

force

wedge

sideways force

A wedge increases the force exerted on the wood and splits apart objects.

This wedge is made of metal. Wedges can also be made of other materials such as wood, stone, or plastic.

Wedges at Work

Wedges change the direction and strength of a force. To split a log, a wedge is placed on the log with its thin edge touching the log. The thick end of the wedge is hit with a **hammer**. The force that hits the thick end of the wedge is **focused** onto the small area touching the log. The wedge cuts into the wood. The wedge also changes the direction of the force from downward to outward. This helps split the log apart. Some wedges are powered by **motors** to drive them deeper into an object.

Saving Effort

Effort is the force needed to do a task. Splitting a log using a wedge requires less effort than splitting it without the wedge. Using a wedge gives us an advantage, which is called a **mechanical advantage**.

Mechanical Advantage

A mechanical advantage is when a machine takes a small **input force** and increases it to make a stronger **output force**. For example, the force from an arm swinging an ax into wood is increased because it is focused on the thin end of the wedge. A small input force on the thicker end of the wedge produces a strong output force on the thinner end.

The narrow wedges laid out on this rock are used to split rock open. The pointed end of each wedge is held on the rock and the thicker end is hit with the hammer.

thick end

wedge

narrow end

Less Effort, Greater Distance

In science, work is defined as a force (effort) **multiplied** by distance. To reduce the force needed to do work, a machine must move a greater distance. A long, thin wedge is easier to push into an object than a short, thick wedge. However, it has to move a greater distance than a short, thick wedge to split the object. A thick, short wedge is harder to push in, but it does not have to move as far to split the object. In both cases, the total amount of work done remains the same. Let's take a look at wedges in action.

wedge

A plow is a type of wedge. Pulling it forward pushes dirt to the side.

See technology in action!

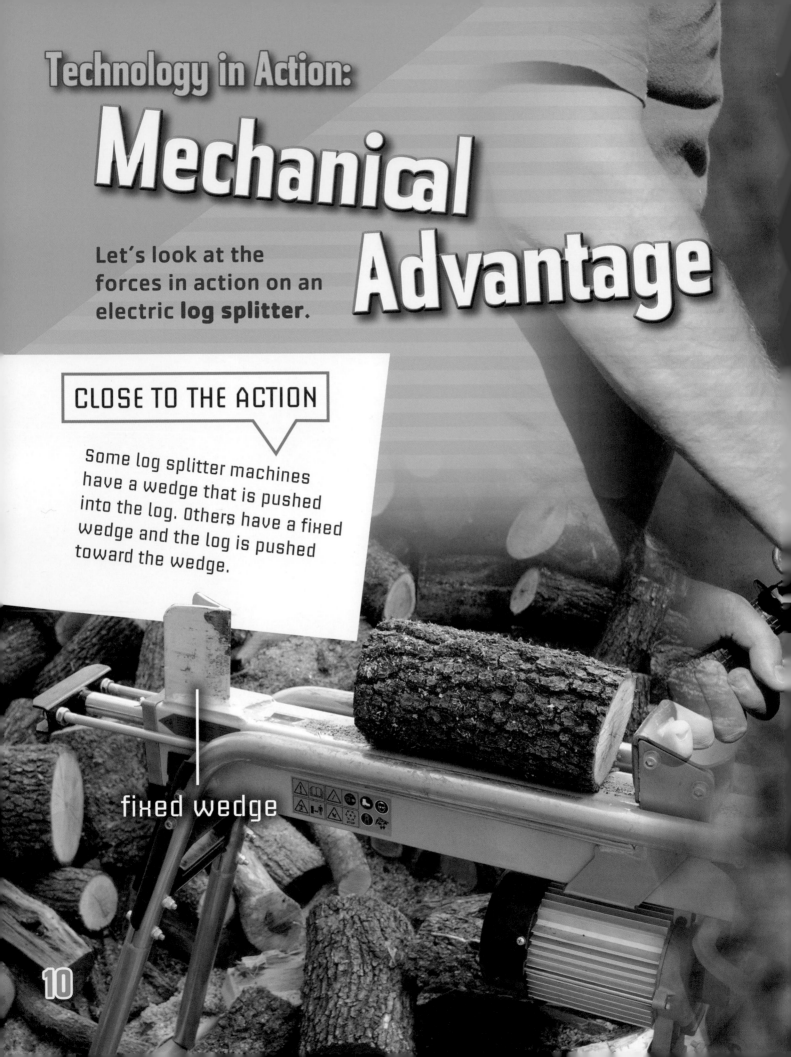

Technology in Action:
Mechanical Advantage

Let's look at the forces in action on an electric **log splitter**.

CLOSE TO THE ACTION

Some log splitter machines have a wedge that is pushed into the log. Others have a fixed wedge and the log is pushed toward the wedge.

fixed wedge

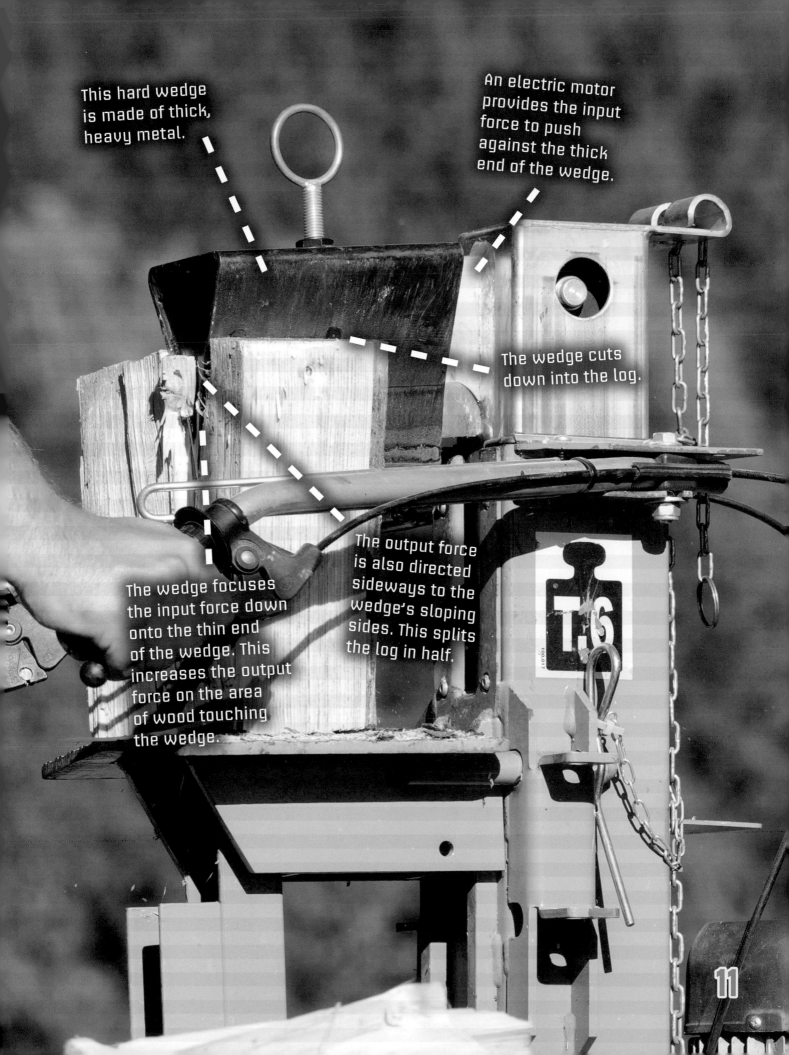

This hard wedge is made of thick, heavy metal.

An electric motor provides the input force to push against the thick end of the wedge.

The wedge cuts down into the log.

The wedge focuses the input force down onto the thin end of the wedge. This increases the output force on the area of wood touching the wedge.

The output force is also directed sideways to the wedge's sloping sides. This splits the log in half.

Moving Apart

Wedges can be used to spread or push apart a lot of different materials, such as wood, snow, and even water.

Wedges to Clear Snow and Ice

Some **snowplows** use a wedge attached to the front of a vehicle to clear snow and ice from roads or railroad tracks. The wedge pushes aside the snow and ice. Snow slides easily over the snowplow's wedge because it has a narrow point and smooth, sloping sides.

This snowplow is a type of wedge. As the train moves forward, the wedge pushes snow to the sides.

— wedge

Many wedge-nosed speedboats can travel at up to 90 miles per hour [145 kmh] on calm water.

wedge

Speedboats

Many speedboats are wedge-shaped to reduce **water resistance** and reach high speeds. Water resistance is the force of the water pushing against the object moving through it, slowing it down. A speedboat with a wedge-shaped **bow** cuts through the water and spreads it apart. A boat designed to reduce water resistance like this is described as **streamlined**. Let's take a look at wedges and forces in action.

See technology in action!

Technology in Action:
Wedges and Force

Let's take a look the forces in action on an **icebreaker**.

This icebreaker has a pointed, wedge-shaped bow.

As the ship moves forward, the wedge cracks open the huge block of floating ice in front of it.

As the ship moves through the ice, the thick end of the wedge shape splits the ice even farther apart.

11

U.

An icebreaker is heavy. This gives it a large input force and an even greater output force to help it cut into thick ice.

CLOSE TO THE ACTION

As well as being shaped like a wedge, an icebreaker's bow is also very strong. It's made of metal that's about 3 feet (1 m) thick.

COAST GUARD

Slicing

Many wedges are used for slicing. These include the knives we use to cut up food and the **scalpels** used by surgeons to carry out surgery on patients.

Sharp Wedges

A knife is a wedge with a very thin, sharp edge. The edge is sharp because there is only a tiny **angle** between the sides of the wedge. This makes the cutting edge of the knife very narrow, which allows it to slice through things easily. When a knife is sharpened, the thin end of the wedge is made even narrower. This increases its mechanical advantage.

The chef presses this knife onto the fish. This force is concentrated on the narrow edge of its wedge and the knife cuts through the fish easily.

This knife is being pulled back along a knife-sharpening block. This block files the thin end of the knife's wedge to make it narrower and sharper.

Long and Short

A carving knife has a long handle and a long, thin blade. This long, thin wedge provides a large mechanical advantage. It concentrates a force applied over a large area on the narrow edge. It is easy to slice the knife into meat, but you have to move the knife a long way forward and backward to do so. A scalpel has a short handle. It requires more force to cut. This reduces the risk of surgeons making a cut that is too long or too deep.

Cutting and Grating

There are other cutting tools that also use one or more wedges. These include **chisels** and cheese graters.

Chisels

A chisel is a tool with a handle and a wedge. Its blade is thick and its two sides have a wide angle. It is used to force apart a section of material and break it off. Artists use chisels to carve statues. Carpenters use chisels to shave chips of wood off a plank. Some chisels use a combination of angles. The edge of the wedge may have one angle for cutting wood, and another angle to push away wood shavings.

blade

This artist is chiseling marble. He hits the chisel with a hammer to force the blade into the marble to cut it.

wedge-shaped cutter

One edge of each of these holes is a wedge-shaped cutter.

Cheese Graters

Cheese graters are made up of multiple, or many, small cutting wedges. As cheese is rubbed along the side, the many wedges on the grater cut off little pieces of cheese. A cheese grater only works in one direction. That is because the cheese must be forced into the cutting edge of the wedge to grate it. Let's take a look at multiple cutting wedges in action!

See technology in action!

Technology in Action:
Multiple Wedges

Let's take a look at multiple cutting wedges in action on a chainsaw.

CLOSE TO THE ACTION

The cutting teeth of a chainsaw are L-shaped. Their sharpest point is where the **vertical** and **horizontal** edges of the "L" meet.

tooth

sharpest point

The **chain** of a chainsaw is made up of many small, sharp wedge-shaped blades called teeth. They are linked together in a long loop.

A motor provides the input force that turns the chain.

As the chain turns, each tooth in turn takes a small bite off the wood.

The chain turns quickly so that the many teeth pass rapidly over the wood. Together, they soon cut through even the thickest tree trunks.

Holding and Lifting

Wedges are not only used for scraping, cutting, slicing, and moving things apart. They can also be used for holding objects together or lifting them up.

Nailing It!

Nails hold pieces of wood together. The tip of a nail is a wedge. When a nail is hit with a hammer, the tip of the nail makes a hole in the wood and pushes it apart. When the nail forces wood **fibers** apart, they try to return to their original position. In doing so, they grip the nail tightly. This keeps the nail from sliding out of the hole.

Before it is hit, the nail is held upright with the thin part of the wedge touching the wood.

wedge

Holding Still and Lifting

A doorstop is a wedge that can hold a door open. When an input force pushes the thick end of a doorstop under a door, the output forces act upward and push on the bottom of the door. This keeps the door from moving. Wedges can also be used to lift objects, by pushing them away from the surface on which they sit. To lift up a box with a forklift, the thin end of a wedge is pushed under the box. The box slides up the sloped side of the wedge and lifts.

This forklift vehicle has wedge-shaped lifting parts.

wedges

Force of Friction

Friction is a force between two surfaces that are moving, or trying to move, across one other. Friction slows a moving object or keeps it from moving at all. Wedges use friction to keep things in one place.

Friction in Action

When a wedge sits between two objects, friction keeps the two objects together. For example, a doorstop stays in place partly because of the friction between the bottom of the door and the doorstop wedge. A nail holds wood together because of friction between the tip of the nail (the wedge) and the fibers of the wood.

The prongs, or tines, on the head of a fork have wedge-shaped ends. When they are inserted in food, friction helps keep the food in place.

wedge

Holding Tight

If a lot of force is used to push two surfaces together, the friction between them will be great. This helps to keep the two surfaces tightly together. Some tent pegs have wedge-shaped ends. When a peg is hammered into the ground, it creates a gap or hole in the ground. The sides of the peg wedge push against the gap. Friction keeps the tent peg in place. Let's look at how wedges and friction work together on aircraft carriers.

Wedge-shaped pegs in the ground hold a tent down, even in bad weather.

See technology in action!

Technology in Action:
Friction and Wedges

Let's take a look at wedges and friction in action on a resting aircraft.

Wedge-shaped stops in front and behind the wheels of a parked aircraft keep it from rolling.

The wedges are jammed hard beneath the wheels. The upward force of the wedges and the force of friction keeps them in position.

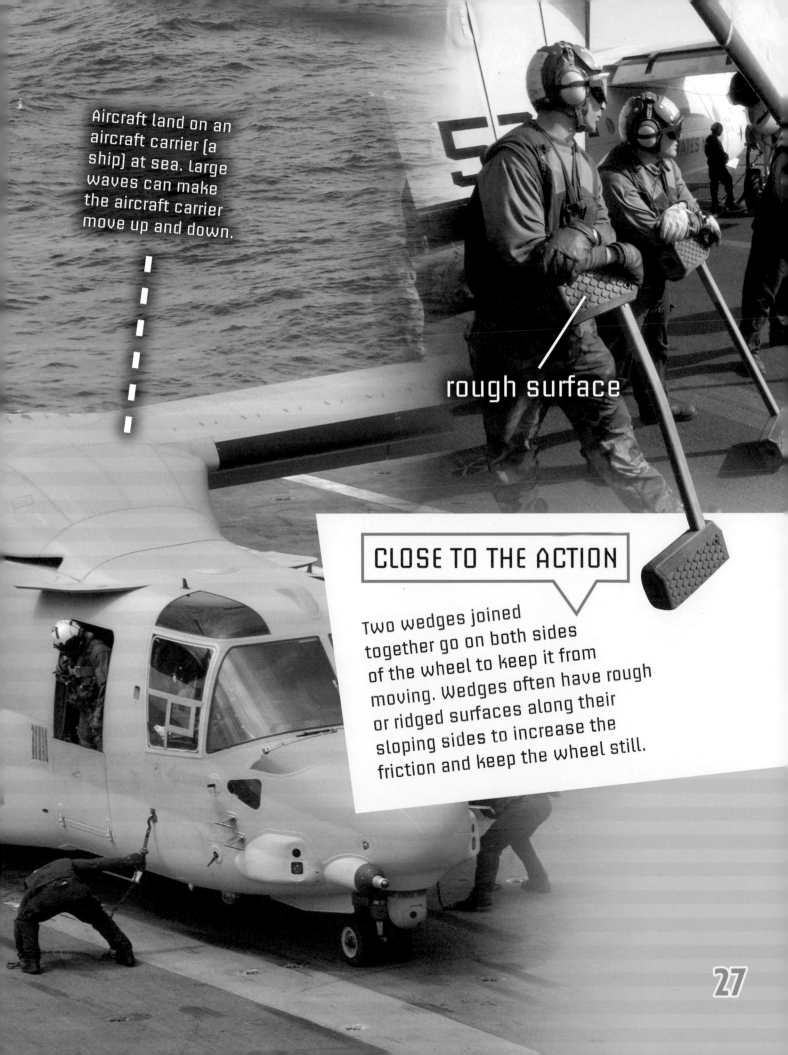

Aircraft land on an aircraft carrier (a ship) at sea. Large waves can make the aircraft carrier move up and down.

rough surface

CLOSE TO THE ACTION

Two wedges joined together go on both sides of the wheel to keep it from moving. Wedges often have rough or ridged surfaces along their sloping sides to increase the friction and keep the wheel still.

Wonderful Wedges

Wedges have been in use for millions of years. Without wedges, early people would not have been able to cut wood, hunt animals, or farm the land.

Wedges of the World

Early humans used wedges made of rocks and stones as arrowheads for hunting. They used wedge axes to cut trees. They used plows to dig the soil. In ancient Egypt, people used metal wedges to break off blocks of stone to build the pyramids. There are even wedges in nature: animal teeth are wedges that cut and slice meat and plants.

This giant coal-mining machine has wedge-shaped cutting scoops that turn to dig huge holes in the ground.

wedge

Sharp teeth are a type of wedge that cut through meat when a crocodile feeds.

Wedges Today

Machines that include two or more simple machines working together are compound machines. Many compound machines contain wedges. Some pencil sharpeners are made up of a wedge with a wheel and axle. In a can opener, the two long arms that hold the can are levers. A wheel and axle is used to rotate the can. The edge of the circular wheel that cuts into the can is a wedge. Wedges are in action all around us!

Glossary

angle The amount of space between two straight lines that have a common end point.

bow The front of a boat.

chain Series of metal rings connected together.

chisels Tools with a thick, wedge-shaped cutting edge. They are hit with a hammer to remove part of a material.

direction The path or line along which something moves or faces.

effort The force used to move something.

fibers Threads or threadlike parts.

focused Directing a lot of something to a particular area.

force A push or a pull.

friction A force that slows down moving objects when they make contact.

hammer A bar with a heavy head used to hit something else.

horizontal Flat and level.

icebreaker A strong, metal ship designed to clear a channel through sea ice.

input force The amount of force used to operate a simple machine.

log splitter A complicated machine that uses a motor to drive a wedge into a log and split it into two.

mechanical advantage The increase of output force relative to input force.

motors Devices that change electricity or fuel into movement and make a machine work.

multiplied Increased in number.

output force The amount of force produced using a simple machine.

ramps Sloping surfaces often joining two different levels.

scalpels Knives with small, sharp blades used by surgeons.

snowplows Vehicles used to clear roads of snow and ice.

streamlined Shaped to move more easily through air or water.

vertical Upright; at right angles to a horizontal surface.

water resistance The push of water against moving things that works to slow them down.

work The force needed to move an object.

Further Reading

BOOKS

Coutts, Lyn. *Machines*. Hauppauge, NY: Barron's Educational Series, 2017.

Miller, Tim, and Rebecca Sjonger. *Wedges in My Makerspace*. New York, NY: Crabtree Publishing Company, 2017.

Rivera, Andrea. *Wedges*. Minneapolis, MN: Abdo Zoom, 2017.

Rustad, Martha E. H. *Wedges*. North Mankato, MN: Capstone Press, 2018.

WEBSITES

Due to the changing nature of Internet links, PowerKids Press has developed an online list of websites related to the subject of this book. This site is updated regularly. Please use this link to access the list: www.powerkidslinks.com/tia/wedges

Index